AUTUMN

LET'S CELEBRATE

WORLD FESTIVALS

Rhoda Nottridge

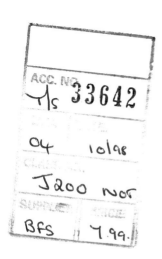

Wayland

Other titles in this series include:

Let's Celebrate Spring
Let's Celebrate Summer
Let's Celebrate Winter

Editor: Deb Elliott
Designer: Helen White

Cover: (top left) Some of the things used in Halloween celebrations: pumpkin lantern, masks and apples. (top right) Dressed in costume for the Nikko autumn festival in Japan. (bottom left) A Guy Fawkes firework display on the banks of the River Thames in London. (bottom right) Celebrating the Diwali festival.

Text is based on *Autumn Festivals* in the *Seasonal Festivals* series published in 1990.

First published in 1994 by
Wayland (Publishers) Limited
61 Western Road, Hove
East Sussex, BN3 IJD, England

© Copyright Wayland (Publishers) Limited

British Library Cataloguing in Publication Data
Nottridge, Rhoda
    Autumn. – (Let's Celebrate Series)
    I. Title II. Series
    394.2

ISBN 0 7502 1180 6

Typeset by White Design
Printed and bound by Casterman S.A., Belgium

CONTENTS

AUTUMN ARRIVES

Autumn is a beautiful time of year. In many parts of the world, the green leaves on trees change colour. They become golden or even red and then they fall off the trees.

BELOW The sun shining on autumn leaves is a beautiful sight.

ABOVE In the countryside autumn is harvest time in many parts of the world.

For animals which sleep through the winter, autumn is a time to find food to eat before they settle down. For farmers it is the last chance they have to pick crops before the winter. Autumn is a time of change and there are many special celebrations.

AN IMPORTANT TIME

People have grown food to eat since early times. In the past, plants sometimes did not grow because they got a disease or bad weather killed them. Every crop of food that grew was very important. If the crop was ruined, people had no food and could die.

BELOW At harvest time everyone on a farm works together to gather in the crops.

ABOVE Fruit picking is hard work, but everyone enjoys celebrating when it is finished.

Making sure that crops grow well is very important. When the food has been safely harvested, people like to celebrate. In the past a good harvest meant there was enough food for the winter, so people were very happy. A good harvest is still important to farmers. For many people autumn is a time when they are thankful so much food has grown during the summer.

HARVEST FESTIVALS

ABOVE In some countries in Asia there are two rice harvests each year. This photograph shows a rice harvest in Bali.

Different kinds of crops are ready at different times of the year. Most fruit and vegetables are ready in the summer. Food such as apples and rice are often the last crops to be harvested in the autumn.

In Britain, the people who work in the London markets have a special parade in autumn. They are called the pearly kings and queens. They celebrate wearing special costumes.

In Germany, the Oktoberfest is a special celebration where people often drink beer made from the newly harvested crops. The festival first started over 200 years ago to celebrate the king's wedding.

LEFT The pearly kings and queens wear special clothes covered in sequins and pearl buttons for their autumn parade.

GIVING THANKS

In the USA and Canada there is a special autumn festival every year. It is called Thanksgiving Day. It began many years ago when European settlers first sailed across the sea to America. When they reached land it was too late in the year to plant any crops. During the winter there was hardly any food for the new settlers and many died.

ABOVE The end of the rice harvest in Japan is a holiday for all workers.

Those people who lived planted seeds the next spring, and at the end of the summer they had a very good harvest. They were so pleased to be alive and to have enough food that they celebrated with a thanksgiving festival.

In Japan there is an important rice harvest in the autumn. None of the rice can be eaten until a special event has happened. There are dances and a procession and a huge feast.

OPPOSITE On Thanksgiving Day, Americans and Canadians celebrate with a special meal of turkey and pumpkin pie.

11

FESTIVALS IN HOT PLACES

ABOVE For a farmer in India the oxen are very important in helping with the harvest. These oxen are decorated for a festival.

In Kerala in South India, people have a special festival called Onam at the end of the rainy season. Everyone cleans their homes and the children go out and pick flowers. The flowers are made into beautiful mats. The children are given new clothes in return for their work. People go to the temple and give thanks for the harvest. Then they have a big meal. After that there are special boat races which everyone enjoys.

In some places in Africa there are religious harvest festivals in the autumn. Some of these festivals have a lot of dancing and music. Some dancers wear masks. Each different dance tells a story. The stories thank good ghosts who have looked after their crops and scare away the bad ghosts who try to spoil the food.

BELOW Music and dancing are an important part of West African harvest festivals.

FESTIVALS OF LIGHT

In autumn the amount of time the sky is light or dark becomes the same. Then winter begins in many parts of the world and the nights become longer and the days get shorter. There is less warmth from the sun. Some ancient peoples had special festivals with torch lights and big bonfires at this time. They believed it helped the sun to keep its strength.

BELOW Jewish people celebrating the Chanukah festival in Israel, with candles burning.

ABOVE Chanukah candles are lit and placed in a special candle holder called a menorah.

Jewish people have a special celebration in early December which uses light. It is called Chanukah. It remembers a time over 2,000 years ago when some Jewish people took back a temple in Jerusalem that had been taken away from them. For every evening of Chanukah, a candle is lit. There are eight evenings, so by the last evening of the festival eight candles burn together.

BONFIRE FESTIVALS

On 5 November every year there is a British festival called bonfire night. On this night nearly 400 years ago, a man called Guy Fawkes tried to blow up everyone in the British government, using gunpowder. He was discovered and put to death. Some people celebrated his death. Since then, many British people have a bonfire and fireworks on bonfire night. They make a model of Guy Fawkes from paper stuffed into old clothes and burn it on the bonfire.

LEFT Before bonfire night, children make a model of Guy Fawkes and ask for money to buy fireworks.

ABOVE *Bonfire celebrations have been held in the autumn for thousands of years.*

Bonfire festivals were held long before Guy Fawkes. Bonfires were part of the old Celtic and other new year festivals. So, when people celebrated the death of Guy Fawkes, it was a reason to carry on having a bonfire in the autumn, even though it was no longer a new year festival.

LEFT *This poster advertises the colourful festival of Diwali in India.*

Diwali is a festival celebrated by Hindus and Sikhs. For Hindus it is the beginning of the new year and for Sikhs it is a time when they remember a very important religious teacher called Guru Hargobind. He had been in prison and was set free.

The festival is held at the end of October or the beginning of November, when there is a new moon.

In the evenings there are wonderful firework displays. In some parts of India people put lamps and candles in the doorways and windows of their homes.

As Diwali is the new year for Hindus, they honour the goddess of prosperity, whose name is Lakshmi. Hindus clean their homes and wear specially washed clothes on Diwali night. They believe the goddess Lakshmi will only visit them and bring them wealth if they have clean homes.

BELOW During Diwali, Hindus tell and act out parts of the ancient story of Rama and Sita.

MOON FESTIVALS

LEFT The moon festival is enjoyed by both adults and children who are in a special parade.

Many ancient calendars are organized around the times of full and new moons. In the autumn, the time of many festivals depends on whether there is a new or full moon.

For the Chinese there is a special moon festival during September. The moon is very special to the Chinese. It is called the Queen of Heaven and women ask for good luck from the moon.

On the evening of the festival, everybody carries around lanterns shaped like animals, birds or fish. People eat little rice cakes shaped like full moons. These moon cakes once played an important part in Chinese history. Over 600 years ago, the Chinese were ruled by the Mongols. They decided to rebel against their rulers. The Chinese hid secret messages in the rice cakes to tell everyone about the rebellion.

LEFT The Chinese make special cakes to eat during the autumn moon festival.

Dassehra and Durga Puja are two Hindu festivals held over ten days in the autumn. They both celebrate the famous ancient story called the Ramayana. At the Dassehra festival, the story is told in a special play, called Ram Lila.

The story tells how Prince Rama's wife, Sita, is taken away by the evil Ravana. After many struggles, Rama rescues Sita and they return to their village.

LEFT These actors are wearing the special costumes worn for the Ram Lila play.

ABOVE Models of the goddess Durga are taken down to the water and set afloat at the end of the Durga Puja festival.

Durga Puja honours the goddess called Durga who helped Rama. During this festival there are dances and parades and performances. People go to the temples to offer the goddess presents of flowers or rice. On the last day of the festival, models of Durga are set afloat on the sea or river.

REMEMBRANCE FESTIVALS

LEFT At Halloween children sometimes wear fancy dress. Pumpkins with holes cut in them and candles inside make frightening faces.

During the autumn new year celebrations, the ancient Celtic peoples remembered their dead. When the Christian religion spread to Celtic countries this caused a problem. The Christians believed that the old Celtic festival was bad. They decided to make a festival of all the Christian saints on 1 November. Some people continued to celebrate on the evening before which became known as Hallow's eve or Halloween.

LEFT In Mexico there is a festival like Halloween which is called the Day of the Dead. People go to graveyards and light candles and say prayers for the dead.

People still enjoy Halloween today, dressing up as ghosts or witches and scaring their friends. In the USA children play a game called 'trick or treat' on Halloween. They knock on a neighbour's door and ask for a treat. If the adult refuses, they play a trick on him or her. This is like the old Celtic idea that if they did not look after the ghosts at the New Year festival, they would play tricks on them.

In Japan, Buddhists remember their dead at the time in autumn of equal days and nights. This is called Higan. It is a time when people visit the graves of friends and family who are dead. They tidy up the area and think about the dead people.

KALI FESTIVAL

LEFT *Images of Kali are put on the streets and people stop to offer her gifts.*

For some Hindus in Bengal there is a special festival in honour of the goddess Kali. Kali is the powerful goddess of death and disease. She is a very frightening goddess. Her followers believe it is important to honour her because death is a part of all life.

LEFT A model of Kali made for the festival.

During the festival of Kali, families or other groups of people make special models of the goddess. She wears a necklace made of skulls and holds her arms upwards. People walk around the streets and visit the models. In the evening they light special lamps by the images and everyone eats special foods.

There are fireworks and then the models are carried down to the river. Everyone sings and bells ring as the images are put on the river and float away. The festival of Kali is then finished for another year.

JEWISH FESTIVALS

For Jewish people there are several important religious times during the autumn. Rosh Hashanah is a two-day festival which begins when there is a new moon.

Many Jewish people go to pray in the morning and evening and have special meals. Part of the meal is a sweet bread called challah. This is dipped in honey to remind people of sweet things that may come to them in the new year.

LEFT During both Rosh Hashanah and Yom Kippur a special musical instrument made out of a ram's horn is played.

ABOVE The day of Yom Kippur has been celebrated for thousands of years. This picture shows some Jews saying prayers on Yom Kippur around 300 years ago.

On the following days, Jews think about the past year. If they have done something wrong they ask for forgiveness. They try to learn from their mistakes and do better in the next year.

After sunset on the ninth day from the beginning of the festival there is a feast. The tenth day is called Yom Kippur. Between sunrise and sunset on Yom Kippur, Jewish people eat nothing. This is to make up for anything wrong they have done and to show that they are serious about not making the same mistakes again.

GLOSSARY

ancient Something that is very old or that happened a long time ago.

celebration A special festival or party when people enjoy their successes.

Celts The ancient peoples who used to live in northern Europe.

costumes Special clothes which people wear when they are dressing up for a festival or special party.

evil Something that is very bad or harmful.

government The people who rule a country.

gunpowder A powder which explodes when it is set alight.

harvest When crops such as fruit and vegetables are gathered or picked.

images Pictures or models which look like people or objects.

prosperity When things go well and people gain wealth or other things.

rebellion When people get together to show that they do not like something.

remembrance Remembering someone who may be dead or absent.

settlers People who move from one place or country and try to live and stay somewhere else.

BOOKS TO READ

Autumn by Ruth Thomson (Watts, 1989)
Faith Stories for Today by Angela Wood
(BBC/Longman 1990)
Harvest Festival by Lynne Hannigan and Renu Nagrath
(A&C Black, 1987)
Hanukkah by Jenny Koralek (Walker Books, 1989)
In Autumn by Ruth Thomson (Watts, 1993)
Poems for Autumn selected by Robert Hull (Wayland,
1990)
Projects for Autumn by Joan Jones (Wayland, 1989)
The Weather in Autumn by Miriam Moss (Wayland,
1994)

Picture acknowledgements
The publishers would like to thank the following for allowing their pictures to be reproduced in this book:

Chapel Studios 13, 18; Das Picture Library 19, 22, 23, 26; Mary Evans Picture Library 29; Eye Ubiquitous cover (top right, Paul Seheult) Hutchison Library cover (bottom left), (bottom right, Liba Taylor), 12, 20, 21, 25; Photri 6, 11, 24; Tony Stone Worldwide 5, 7; Topham Picture Library 9, 10, 16, 17; ZEFA cover (top left), 4, 8, 14, 15, 28.

INDEX